DRIFT BOTTLES

in History and Folklore

DRIFT BOTTLES
in History and Folklore

WRITTEN BY
Dorothy B. Francis

ARTWORK BY
Kate McGowan Schultz

Published by

BALLyhoo BOOKS
P.O. Box 534
Shoreham, NY 11786

DRIFT BOTTLES in History and Folklore

Text: Copyright © 1990 by Dorothy B. Francis
Illustrations: Copyright © 1990 by BALLYHOO BOOKS

First Printing: May, 1990

ISBN: 0-936335-02-5

Library of Congress Cataloging-in-Publication Data

    Francis, Dorothy Brenner.
      Drift bottles in history and folklore.

      Includes bibliographical references.
      Summary: An illustrated history of drift bottles from ancient Greece to modern times, including un-usual facts and anecdotes about their role in history, love, war, and scientific discovery.
      1. Drift bottles--Juvenile literature. [1. Drift bottles. 2. Ocean bottles] I. Schultz, Kate McGown, 1951-   ill. II. Title.
    G532.F726 1990   302.2'244   90-493
    ISBN 0-936335-02-5

Thanks to: Shelley Lantheaume of Camera Ready Typesetters
              Robert Parisi of R.J.P. Graphics
Book design: Brian J. Heinz
Photographs: Brian J. Heinz

Printed in the United States of America   ISBN: 0-936335-02-5

For Richard

REWARD ☆ № 12157

REMOVE CARD FROM BOTTLE, PLEASE FILL IN INFORMATION
AS INDICATED, AND SEND BY MAIL

Where found (name of beach or place on shore, near what Coast Guard
station, Lighthouse, or other prominent reference point) ....
....

When found, date ....

Your Name (print) ....

Your Home Address (print) ....
....
....

Your return will assist the addressee in a study of coastal circulation.
Fifty cents plus location and date of release will be sent to finder on return of this card.

CHAPTERS

A MESSAGE FROM THE SEA

Have you ever dreamed of finding a sealed bottle with a message inside? You might see it in a river or a sea. You might find it buried on a sandy shore. It could be almost hidden behind some rocks.

Imagine opening such a bottle. Would you remove the cap? What if that cap was stuck? Would you break the bottle? What would you do?

The message inside a drift bottle might help find a missing person. It might solve the mystery of a sunken Spanish galleon. Such a message could lead the finder to adventure and excitement. It's fun to dream about such things.

For ages people have tossed message bottles into the sea. Sometimes these bottles are called drift bottles. They also are called *drogues*. A drogue is another name for a container used at sea.

Ancient Greeks learned about water currents by using drift bottles. One Greek writer wrote of using drogues 300 years before Christ's birth. He stood on a seawall in Athens. From there, he dropped drift bottles into the water. Each bottle carried a message. The message asked the finder to contact the writer. These bottles helped him learn about the flow of sea currents.

As far back as 300 B.C., a Greek writer wrote of using drogues, or drift bottles.

Through the centuries many people have used drogues. An English fisherman opened a sealed bottle he netted from the surf. The bottle carried a secret report. A British sea captain had written it. He was sending it to the queen of England.

The fisherman almost lost his life for uncapping the bottle. Only his ignorance saved him. He proved that he could neither read nor write. He knew nothing about drift bottle laws.

At that time, there were no telephones. There were no telegraphs. Mail traveled slowly between ship and shore. It was hard for a sailor to deliver a message quickly.

Queen Elizabeth I took the use of drift bottles very seriously. She appointed an Official Uncorker of Ocean Bottles. Such bottles bore an official naval seal. It was against the law for a private citizen to open such a bottle. British courts upheld the drift bottle laws for 200 years.

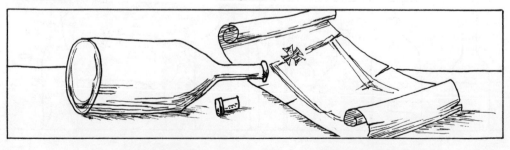

Queen Elizabeth I, appointed an Official Uncorker of Ocean Bottles.

Even Ben Franklin was interested in drift bottles. He was Postmaster General for the American colonies. Mail traveled between England and the colonies by ship.

Franklin noted something strange about mail delivery. It took letters a long time to reach America from England. But, it took two weeks longer for them to reach England from America. Why, Franklin wondered. The ships traveled the same route. Surely the ocean didn't change in size.

Benjamin Franklin. From History of the World, Little and Weber, P.W. Ziegler and Co., 1894.

Benjamin Franklin used drift bottles to measure and map sea currents in the Gulf Stream.

Franklin was curious. He was a thinker. He studied the mail question. He found no answer until he talked with his cousin. This man was a Nantucket whaling captain. He told Franklin about the Gulf Stream.

The Gulf Stream is an ocean current. It is so strong it has been called a river in the sea. Whaling captains knew about the Gulf Stream.

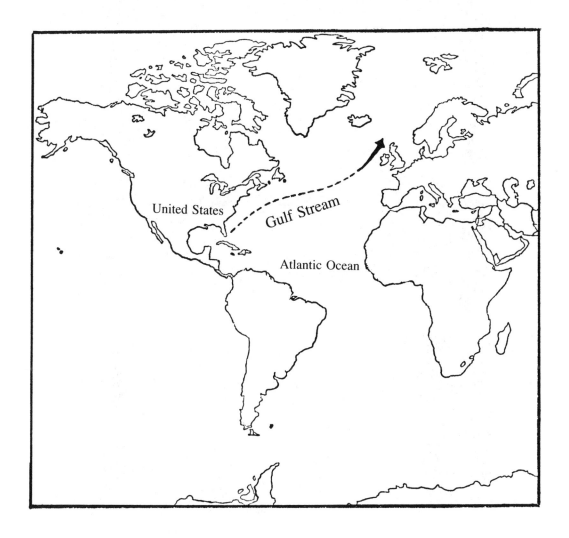

Smart ship captains sailed directly across the Gulf Stream. Those who didn't were sorry. They wasted time and effort fighting the strong current.

Once Franklin learned about the Gulf Stream, he took action. He had a map drawn that marked this current. He asked whaling captains to drop message bottles into this stream. They were glad to help.

The captains of whaling ships helped Benjamin Franklin with his drift bottle experiments.

Franklin received many replies. They helped him measure sea currents. At last he had found a way to speed up the mail. He sent his findings to England, but they were ignored. Nobody listened to him. You can imagine his disappointment. The mail between England and America continued to travel slowly.

The use of message bottles is not all history. The United States Government uses drogues today. The messages they contain provide facts on sea currents. If you live near the sea, watch for drift bottles. You might find one containing a message. Many people do.

If you find such a bottle, handle it with care. The message may be from the U.S. Coast and Geodetic Survey. These scientisits continue to study ocean currents. The bottle you find may contain a form. If so, fill it out and return it. You may get a small reward for your help.

WHAT IS GLASS?

Why would anyone place an important message in a glass bottle? Remember the window pane you broke? You only hit it gently with a rubber ball. And what about Aunt Mary's goblet? You didn't drop it. You just barely bumped it against the sink. But it cracked and shattered. How can a fragile glass container survive in the roaring sea?

What is this substance called glass? Maybe it is stronger than it seems. Glass is made mostly of sand. Soda ash or a similar chemical must be mixed with the sand. This mixture must be heated to a high temperature. When it is very hot, the soda ash makes the sand melt. When the mixture cools, no crystals are formed. The result is glass.

Glass has been on earth for millions of years. Nature created glass in two ways. In one way, lightning struck sand. The great heat from the lightning melted the sand. This action formed slender glass tubes called fulgurites.

In another way, nature used the heat in volcanoes to make glass. Again, the sand was melted at a high temperature. This sort of glass is called obsidian.

Humans used nature's glass for many years. They made tools, weapons, and ornaments from obsidian. Some obsidian pieces have been dated thousands of years before Christ. Then people learned to make glass for themselves.

The art of glass making is over 3,000 years old. The first man-made glass was a glaze. It was made from mixing heated sand and minerals. The mixture was fused to stone or clay in an oven. The result was a glazed dish or ornament. As early as 1300 B.C. Egyptians were making small glass vessels.

Artisans developed methods of glass blowing 1,000 years before Christ. Romans were the first glass blowers. They learned to lift a limp of soft glass onto a hollow iron rod. By blowing into the rod, they created useful objects. Some vases, bottles, and dishes date back to Roman times.

The ancient art of glass blowing to create bottles is still practiced today.

Glass blowing made it possible to produce useful items quickly. This are spread from country to country. Bottles were some of the first blown-glass items produced.

Today, glass is made in many ways. Mixtures of the 102 elements in the earth's surface are used. You might compare making glass to making candy. Pretend the sand is sugar. Pretend the soda ash that makes the sand melt is water. Other ingredients may be added. Then the mixture is heated until it is done.

There are many kinds of candy. You can probably name quite a few that are your favorites. There are also many kinds of glass. Glass makers know of about 20,000 different kinds.

Glass may be very fragile while it's on land. But at sea glass is quite durable. Sealed bottles make seaworthy vessels. They can outlive storms. Because they are lightweight, they can survive waves that would capsize ships.

A sturdy glass bottle of any shape can work well as a drift bottle.

Stories of unbroken drift bottles sometimes boggle the mind. In 1954, eighteen bottles washed ashore on England's Kent Coast. The bottles contained no messages. Inside was only a dark smelly liquid. Scientists examined the bottles and their contents in detail. They declared them to be beer bottles. They learned that the ship they came from sank about 250 years ago. The bottles survived all those years in good condition. The beer did not.

About 200 years ago, Japanese treasure hunters sailed the South Seas. They were shipwrecked on an uninhabited island. They had no food or water. One man, Chunosoke Matsuyama, wanted people to know what had happened. He wrote a message telling of their plight. He sealed the message in a bottle and dropped it into the sea.

This man's message bottle drifted for 150 years without breaking. It is sad that nobody found the message sooner. It might have led to the rescue of the treasure hunters. When this bottle washed ashore, it was near the village where Matsuyama had lived.

Chunosoke Matsuyama's message of distress drifted for 150 years before it was found near the village where he had lived.

In 1912, a huge ship named the *Titanic* hit an iceberg. the ship sank in very deep water. There were some survivors, but many lives were lost. At that time, nobody dreamed of finding the vessel or its contents. But diving methods improved. Salvage methods and equipment also improved.

Salvagers and scientists remembered the *Titanic*. Divers recently discovered the vessel on the sea bottom. Much of it had been destroyed. But on the seabed nearby, they found undamaged bottles of wine.

The Titanic hit an iceberg and sunk in 1912. Recently, undamaged bottles of wine were found on the sea bottom near the wreck.

11

Glass is not like metal or wood. It does not corrode when left in water for years. It does not rot and break into fragments. A glass bottle makes a perfect container for ocean mail. All that is necessary is some ballast and a proper seal.

ROMANCE

Some drift bottles have carried scientific surveys. Others have contained military messages. The notes in some drogues have concerned matters of the heart.

In the 1950's, Aake Viking worked as a merchant seaman. He sailed on ships out of Gothenburg, Sweden. Merchant seamen are hard-working sailors. But sometimes they have free time. Aake had some extra minutes while he was sailing in the Mediterranean Sea. There is little entertainment aboard a working ship. Perhaps Aake became bored.

For something to do, he prepared a message bottle and tossed it into the waves. The message was addressed to: **All Girls Between 16 and 20.** The note was short.

"If you want to marry a handsome, blonde Swede, please write." Of course, Aake included his name and address. And, once back at work, he probably forgot all about the bottle. That was not the end of it, though.

The bottle appeared two years later in Sicily. A factory worker tramping along a deserted beach found it. What is this, he thought. He picked it up and examined it. At last he broke it open and found the message. A typical sailor's joke, he thought. But he took the note home.

Paolina, his daughter, liked the message. Deciding to go along with the joke, she wrote to Aake. In time, he responded. Soon many letters were traveling between Sweden and Sicily.

In a few months the pair began discussing marriage. They became man and wife in Sicily, in the fall of 1958.

The marriage of Aake and Paolina was the result of a drift bottle message.

Historians tell of another drift bottle that led to a romance. When a British sailor saw a floating bottle, he retrieved it. The message was a simple one. "Fate, bring me a wife." The writer enclosed his name and address.

The sender's wish was granted. One of the ship's stewardesses replied to the note. Eventually, she accepted the writer's proposal.

Message bottles can change lives.

★★★★★★★★★★★★

OCEAN MAIL

When you write a letter, do you expect a quick reply? Most of us do. Or at least we hope for one. If the sea is to be your postman, be patient. Your reply could arrive in a few days. But it might take weeks, months, or years. Or you may receive no reply at all.

You've already read of two cases when ocean mail traveled very slowly: The Swedish sailor waited two years to hear from his future wife. The Japanese treasure hunter's message wasn't found for 150 years. There are other amazing accounts of bottles. Many have drifted for years before they were found.

About 30 years ago, a bottle washed ashore in Tasmania, an island south of the Australian mainland. The message inside carried a 1916 date. Two men had signed the note. Those were war years. These men wrote that they were on a troopship. Their ship was bound for France.

The message finder became interested in this note. He managed to locate the mother of one of the men. She identified the writing as that of her son. He had been killed during World War I in 1918.

In 1916, two men launched a drift bottle from their troopship bound for France. It was found over forty years later on the shore of Tasmania.

Sometimes bottle messages travel swiftly. They may reach their destinations almost as quickly as letters mailed at the post office. In 1981, California students were helping scientists. Their goal was to trace the paths of ocean currents. The students helped prepare drift bottle messages. From a ship they launched 2,000 bottles off the coast near San Diego.

Only five days later, the first bottle was found. An eight-year-old California boy was fishing in Mexico. He saw a floating bottle and pulled it ashore. He could see and read instructions through the glass. Following these instructions, he reported his find to "National Geographic World." People at this magazine's office were keeping track of the bottles found. They welcomed the boy's quick response.

Few of the bottles were found as quickly as this first one. Six months later, only 207 finders returned cards from these drogues. The cards arrived from the United States, Mexico, and the Philippine Islands. Many of the bottles were never found.

What happened to the bottles that were never heard from? One can only guess. Perhaps some were found, but the finder did not reply. It's more likely that the bottles weren't found. Waves could have shattered them against rocks. Storms could have buried them in sand. Or they may be on an uninhabited shore still waiting for discovery.

A Miami man decided to add some local color to his restaurant. He launched message bottles nearby in the Gulf Stream. In just several weeks, answers began to arrive. This man has decorated one of his dining rooms with these responses. Replies have arrived from all along the coast of Europe. Customers enjoy reading these messages when they visit his restaurant.

Recently, a photographer from Bartlesville, Oklahoma traveled to Texas. He was taking pictures on an oil rig in the Gulf of Mexico. The vast expanse of water inspired him. He dropped a message bottle into the waves. He gave his name and address, asking the finder to contact him.

At his home a week later, this man received a phone call. A couple visiting Padre Island, Texas had found his message bottle. Their response elated him. A surprise came when he asked the caller where he lived. This man also was from Bartlesville. He lived two miles from the man who had launched the message.

Another case tells of a boy receiving a quick reply to a bottle message. This boy lived in Beirut, Lebanon. His father worked there with the United States Embassy. The child was sometimes lonely and he wanted a pen pal. Being a creative person, he sought one by means of a drift bottle.

Within a month he had his pen pel. His message had been found. An eleven-year-old boy replied by postal mail. His letter came from Antiparos, a tiny island miles away in the Aegean Sea.

If you want a speedy reply, mail your messages at the post office. If you're in no hurry, drop your message into the sea. You may receive no reply. Or you may receive a message you'll always remember.

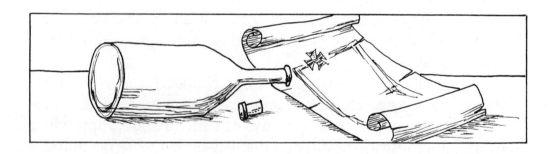

HYDROGRAPHERS

The word hydrographer (hi-drog'-ra-fer) is a big one. Don't let it scare you. Break it into shorter segments. Hydro refers to water. Graph refers to a chart or a map. So a hydrographer is a person who makes sea maps. He charts the surface waters of seas and oceans.

A hydrographer can be a professional who gets paid for his work. Or he can be an amateur. Amateurs pursue the occupation as an interesting and useful hobby.

Do hydrographers have all the answers concerning drift bottles? They probably do not. Why do some bottles drift for years? Why are other bottles found within days? Hydrographers have some of the answers. They can truthfully reply, "It's due to ocean currents."

Professional hydrographers use drogues as the Greeks used them centuries ago. The U.S. Hydrographic Office is our busiest message-in-a-bottle user.

Each year hydrographers from this office launch several thousand message bottles. Not everyone understands English or Spanish. So inside each bottle is a message translated in eight languages. Each year about 400 of these bottles are found. Reports come in from all over the world.

Florida's Department of Natural Resources conducted scientific cruises in the 1960's. They lasted over a period of 28 months. This research series was called the Hourglass cruises. The purpose was to study the speed of ocean surface currents.

Hydrographers chose 16 places (called stations) in the sea to study. Drift bottles were released at regular times from each station. These researchers kept careful records. They recorded the release and recovery of thousands of drogues.

19

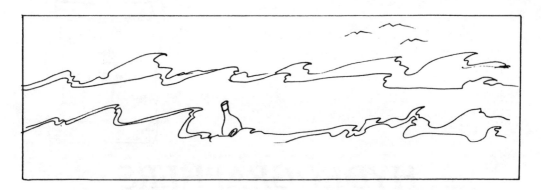

In this study, they used eight-ounce bottles of clear glass. The bottles contained no ballast, or weight. They were sealed with corks. Inside each bottle was a stamped, self-addressed card. Many Spanish speaking people lived in the area. Reply cards bore printing in both English and Spanish.

The words 'BREAK THIS BOTTLE' were easily seen through the glass. You may wonder why the hydrographers wanted the bottles broken. They had good reason for this request.

Anyone removing the card through the neck of the bottle might tear it. A tear could destroy the file number on the card. If that happened, valuable information would be lost.

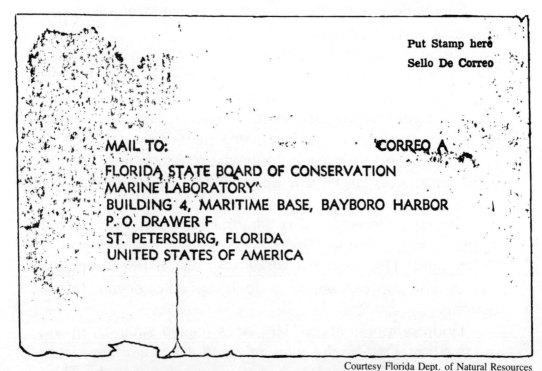

Put Stamp here
Sello De Correo

MAIL TO: CORREO A

FLORIDA STATE BOARD OF CONSERVATION
MARINE LABORATORY
BUILDING 4, MARITIME BASE, BAYBORO HARBOR
P. O. DRAWER F
ST. PETERSBURG, FLORIDA
UNITED STATES OF AMERICA

Courtesy Florida Dept. of Natural Resources

Cards from drift bottles are sometimes returned in poor condition.

The drift bottle message asked the finder to answer some questions. These questions concerned when and where the bottle had been found. Then the finder was to mail the card to the laboratory. The hydrographers offered no reward. Each person who returned a card received a letter of thanks.

REWARD		☆ №	**12157**

REMOVE CARD FROM BOTTLE, PLEASE FILL IN INFORMATION
AS INDICATED, AND SEND BY MAIL

Where found (name of beach or place on shore, near what Coast Guard station, Lighthouse, or other prominent reference point) ....
....

When found, date ....

Your Name (print) ....

Your Home Address (print) ....
....
....

Your return will assist the addressee in a study of coastal circulation.
Fifty cents plus location and date of release will be sent to finder on return of this card.

Courtesy Florida Dept. of Natural Resources

Drift bottle data were recorded. Hydrographers studied dates of bottle release and recovery. The largest percentage of bottles were found stranded on beaches. The amount of coastline development was important to the study. Bottles cast onto a Miami beach might be found quickly. Bottles washing onto an uninhabited shore might not be found for years.

Hydrographers faced other problems. A bottle might wash ashore then be refloated by the next tide. Or, a bottle might be buried by sand and wind action. Mangrove trees grow along much of Florida's coastline. Drift bottles could be trapped in mangrove roots.

Drift bottles can be trapped in mangrove tree roots or buried in the sand.

During the Hourglass cruises 4,460 drift bottles were released. About one third of them were recovered. This was a very high percentage. Records show that less than 10% of all drogues are recovered.

Many people enjoy the beaches in sunny climates. Researchers believe these areas are good for releasing drift bottles. People are likely to find and return them. Favorite recovery areas are the Caribbean Sea, the Gulf of Mexico, and South Florida.

Data from the Hourglass cruises proved valuable. Hydrographers recorded much needed information. This data concerned the ocean's surface circulation in the Gulf of Mexico. This information will be valuable to people who travel the seas. It will benefit those who are involved in sea-related activities.

★★★★★★★★★★★★

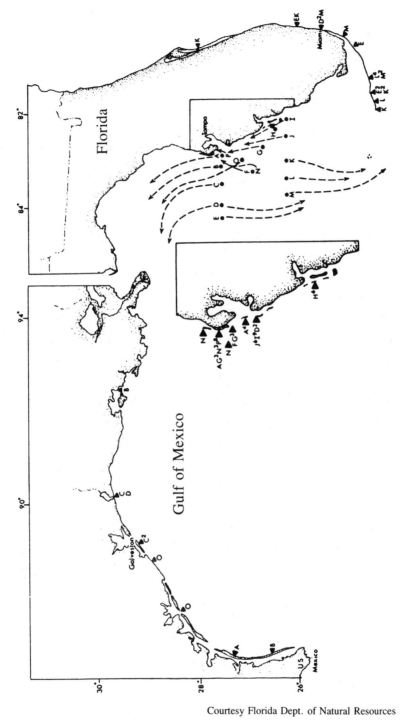

Courtesy Florida Dept. of Natural Resources

Scientists produced maps like this as a result of drift bottle information from the Hourglass Cruises.

THE AMATEURS

Amateur hydrographers seldom are paid for their work. They experiment with drift bottles for personal pleasure. Their interest may be a one-time thing. Or it may be a continued activity.

Many amateurs just want to receive a reply from a drift bottle message. Will anyone find it? If so, who? Where? Will the finder respond? Releasing message bottles is fun. It stirs the imagination. It arouses one's curiosity.

Using drift bottles also makes a person more observant. He notices details. That bit of glass protruding from the sand might carry a message. It's fun to toss drogues into the sea. But it also would be fun to find one someone else had set adrift. The amateur hydrographer looks carefully at bottles washed ashore.

Fishermen are primarily after fish. But they may use drift bottles to secure information about those fish. A group of drift bottles could help them locate new and better fishing grounds. It could help them chart the route of storms. Drift bottle information could help a seaman avoid hurricanes.

Fishermen can use drift bottle information to find new fishing grounds or to chart the path of storms.

Fishermen dread 'red tides', tides that carry poisonous matter. These tides kill marine life. Sometimes drift bottle information can warn where the next 'red tide' will strike.

In 1937, amateur hydrographers used drift bottles to solve a mystery. The people of Long Island, New York had a garbage problem. It wasn't their garbage that was troubling them. Instead, it was garbage that drifted onto their southern beaches.

Swimmers disliked sharing the waves with floating grapefruit peelings. Picnickers avoided beaches that were cluttered with ham bones and egg shells. Boaters hated the smell of rotting vegetables. Where was this garbage coming from! People wanted to know who was responsible for it. They wanted to know what could be done about it.

Some amateur hydrographers had an idea. They helped solve the mystery by using drift bottles. City officials dropped 400 message bottles into the sea. They chose a point about 25 miles southeast of Long Island. About 20 percent of the bottles returned to Long Island shores. This high percentage of returns helped spot the culprit.

Perhaps the hydrographers had suspected the answer all along. Ships were using the sea off Long Island as a dumping ground. Ship captains were unaware of the problem they had caused. A change in dumping sites cooled hot tempers. People again could enjoy the beaches.

Prince Albert I of Monaco was an enthusiastic amateur hydrographer. He used many bottled messages to chart sea currents. He kept his charts up to date and accurate. After World War I, his charts proved valuable. At that time explosive mines still drifted off the coast of Europe. Prince Albert's maps helped ship captains avoid them.

Following World War II, dangerous mines were floating in the Pacific Ocean. Both human lives and valuable ships were in danger. Drift bottle studies helped sea captains avoid these devices. The studies had been made by American and Japanese amateur hydrographers.

Drift bottle studies helped ships avoid deadly, explosive sea mines after World War II.

Some people like to launch drift bottles as a hobby. One California couple asks friends who go on cruises to help them. Vacationers bound for Australia launched a dozen message bottles for this pair.

The first reply came within a month from the Fiji Islands. This couple's hobby has grown over the years. They now have a worldwide list of pen pals.

Whether hydrographers are amateurs or professionals, their use of drift bottles captures the imagination.

7

THE LONGEST TRIP

Sometimes drift bottles are found quickly. They may have traveled a great distance, but they did it in a hurry. Perhaps the wind and waves of a storm help them along. Surely they came to rest on a much-used beach. People must have spotted them easily.

Other times, drift bottles move very slowly. They may come to rest on an uninhabited island. They are found years after they were dropped into the sea.

Finders of such old drift bottles usually wonder where the bottle has been. Maybe it was cast ashore for all those years. Or maybe it has been floating on the waves for decades.

About sixty years ago, German hydrographers made a test. They wanted to learn how far and how long a drogue would float. They prepared a special bottle. A finder could read it without breaking the glass.

The message included the name and address of the German scientific team. They asked anyone finding the bottle to reply. They wanted to know when and where the bottle was found. They also asked the finder to replace the bottle in the sea. That is a lot to ask of strangers. The team offered no reward to the finder. They provided no stamped and addressed reply card. But an aura of mystery and excitement surrounds drift bottles. Many finders responded to the team's request.

These scientists first launched their bottle in the south Indian Ocean. The location was somewhere between the Kerguelen Islands and Tasmania. As they had hoped, answers began to come in.

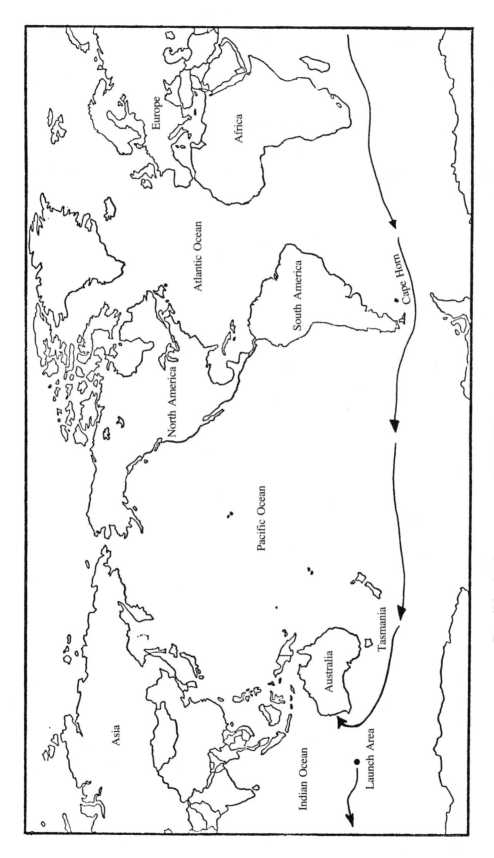

Possibly the longest recorded drift bottle trip lasted 2,447 days, almost seven years. The bottle traveled an estimated 16,800 nautical miles.

The replies showed that the bottle had drifted eastward. It reached the tip of South America. It rounded Cape Horn, drifting into the South Atlantic. From there it found its way back to the Indian Ocean. The team ended the experiment when the bottle washed ashore in western Australia.

This drift bottle traveled an estimated 16,800 nautical miles. Its journey lasted 2,447 days, or almost seven years. This is believed to be the most miles recorded for any drift bottle.

BELIEVE IT OR NOT

Many stories concerning drift bottles are almost beyond belief. Others boggle the mind, to say the least. Consider the following true incidents.

In 1924, Boyle Branscum, an Arkansas boy, made a drift bottle. Inside it, he sealed a picture of himself. In the picture he was wearing his school's basketball uniform.

Branscum lived far from the sea. So, he tossed his bottle into a river. Years passed and he heard nothing from his drift message. He probably forgot all about it. But during all those years, the message kept floating.

In this country there is an imaginary line. It is called the Continental Divide. Rivers west of this line flow into the Pacific Ocean. Rivers east of this line flow into the Atlantic Ocean. Boyle Branscum lived east of the Continental Divide. The river he tossed his bottle into flowed into the Atlantic Ocean.

One day Branscum's message washed ashore at Key Largo, Florida. A young man named Bill Headstream found it. Upon opening it, he could hardly believe what he saw. He recognized the boy in the picture. He recognized that school basketball uniform. He recognized Branscum's address on the back of the picture.

Believe it or not, Boyle Branscum, had been Bill Headstream's pal. They had not seen each other since school days. The address helped reunite the friends who had not met for 25 years.

Sometimes people on a sinking ship toss a message into the sea. Their drogue may be a cry for help. Or it may just be an account of the disaster. The victim may want people to know exactly what happened. His message may concern himself, his friends, and his ship.

One man aboard the British transport ship *Kent* wrote of its disaster. Major Duncan MacGregor knew his ship was in big trouble. It was going down. Nothing short of a miracle could save it. He doubted that anyone would survive to tell the tale.

He wrote an account of the wreck. Hoping someone would find it, he launched his story sealed in a bottle. Luckily, rescuers reached Major MacGregor. Once he was saved, his message bottle seemed less important. He was able to tell his story in person.

Major MacGregor lived in Barbados. He seldom thought of the bottle he had cast into the waves. But nine years after the *Kent* disaster, a servant approached him. The servant carried a bottle. Inside it was the message the major had tossed into the sea.

Believe it or not, the bottle had traveled more than 5,000 miles. It had washed ashore close to the major's doorstep. The sea takes. And the sea returns.

Most ministers speak from a church pulpit. A Tacoma, Washington minister also preached by using drift bottles.

Starting in 1960, this minister released thousands of drift bottles. What kind? Whiskey and wine bottles were his choice. Inside each bottle he included his name and address. He also inserted short Gospel messages. And sometimes he wrote warnings concerning the dangers of liquor.

This minister received many replies to his drift bottle notes. Some writers agreed with him. Others disagreed. One person responded in anger. He was a distiller, a maker of whiskey. Believe it or not!

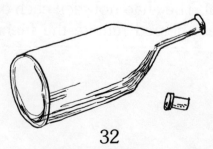

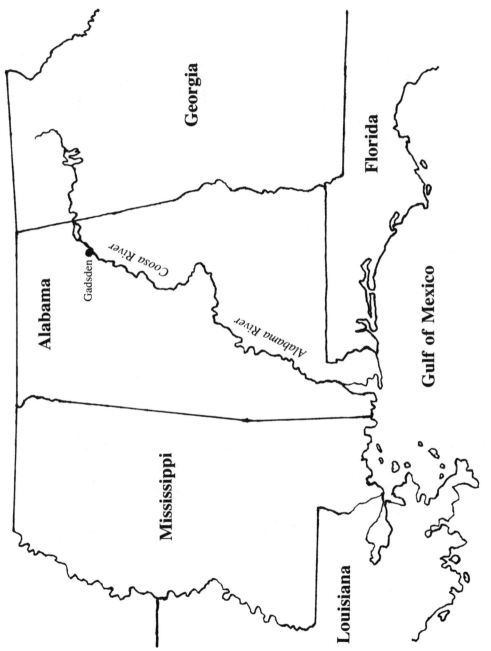

A part-time preacher from Gadsden, Alabama tossed whiskey bottle drogues into the Coosa River. The bottles were carried to the Gulf of Mexico and into the Atlantic Ocean. He received over 5,000 replies from 29 states and 10 foreign countries.

Another reformer worked out of Gadsden, Alabama. He was a full-time textile clerk and a part-time preacher. For over 20 years he worked at an unusual hobby. He spent his Sunday afternoons tossing liquor bottles into the Coosa River. Inside each bottle a message warned the finder of the evils of drink.

The Coosa River was a long one. It flowed for 400 miles before it entered the Gulf of Mexico. Many of this man's bottles reached the sea. He received over 5,000 replies to his messages. They came from 29 states and 10 foreign countries.

One letter scolded him for meddling in other peoples' affairs. That message came from a local Alabama bootlegger, a person who makes illegal whiskey. Believe it or not.

PUBLICITY STUNTS

The finders and senders of drift bottles may receive media notice. These people may make newspaper headlines. Some may be invited to appear on radio and television shows. Business people sometimes seek such publicity. They know the value of using drift bottles in advertising.

In 1958, an Australian department store had a birthday. This store had been in business for 120 years. To celebrate the occasion, store officials set gift-bearing drift bottles afloat. And of course they organized an advertising campaign. They wanted the public to know of the event.

People of all ages suddenly grew interested in beach activities. They combed nearby shores looking for drift bottles.

Each advertising bottle contained a gift certificate. The certificates amounted to a total of $12,500. The publicity staff knew that very few bottles would be recovered. It was an inexpensive way of celebrating and advertising.

Another publicity stunt took place in New York City. Officials at a radio station were trying to draw more listeners. They made an unusual announcement.

They told their audience that they were giving away $1,000. It would be a lump-sum gift. The person finding the money got to keep it. Of course there was a slight catch to all this. But it was that catch which caught the public's interest.

Listeners learned that the money had been placed in a sealed bottle. The bottle then had been cast into New York Harbor. You can guess what happened next.

Throngs of people combed the wharfs and beaches looking for the bottle. Boat owners readied their crafts. They searched nooks and crannies of the harbor for that floating fortune.

Listeners also stayed tuned to that radio station. They wanted to know who, when and where details. Had someone found the bottle? Was there really $1,000 in it?

The bottle remained in the sea. Long after the advertising promotion had been forgotten, the bottle turned up. A farm boy living in the far-distant Azores found it. The lad was $1,000 richer although he had never owned a radio.

In 1959, these drift bottles came ashore on Fire Island, New York. They were part of a publicity campaign by the Guiness brewery in the British Isles. The bottles were embossed with designs and these words:

Special Bottle Drop
(Atlantic Ocean)
To Celebrate and Commemorate the Guiness Bicentenary
1759-1959

Inside were a map and two promotional advertisements.

The bottles were sealed with tarred tape and fitted with a special lead cap which wrapped over the neck.

People often seek fame and publicity. Sometimes they know it won't make them any richer. Daisy Singer Alexander was such a person. Sewing machine millionaire, Isaac Singer, left a fortune to his daughter, Daisy.

Daisy, for unknown reasons, placed her will in a drift bottle. She left her $12 million dollar fortune to two people. The first person was her lawyer. The second lucky person would be the one who found the drift bottle.

A dozen years passed. Nobody showed up with Daisy's will. Then, a year later, a poor dishwasher found the bottle. His lucky find made him a rich man overnight.

From this will-in-the-bottle caper, Daisy has gained fame of sorts. Her name still lives in the memory of many drift bottle buffs.

Most Americans have heard of Charles A. Lindberg. This daring aviator earned the nickname Lucky Lindy. He made the first solo flight across the Atlantic Ocean. The year was 1927.

People went wild at the news of Lindy's successful flight.

A wealthy man sailing aboard the luxury liner *President Roosevelt* wanted to celebrate. He flung a money-filled bottle into the sea. It was his tribute to Lindberg. Of course, he didn't use coins. They would have been too heavy. The money was in the form of a check.

Some time later, a French seamstress found the bottle. It had washed ashore in Morocco. Yes, the check was good. The seamstress must have considered herself almost as lucky as Lindy.

Are you thinking of using a drift bottle as a publicity stunt? Think about it carefully. The sea may cast your bottle on distant shores. Or the waves may return it almost to your doorstep.

But one thing is for certain. The sea offers no guarantees as to time and place of delivery. You may never see or hear of your bottle again.

WELCOME TO
THE UNITED STATES

In 1979, the John Peckhams took a Christmas cruise. They traveled from their home in Los Angeles to Hawaii. The idea of drift bottles caught their imaginations. While aboard ship they experimented with a message bottle of their own.

Inside their bottle the Peckhams enclosed their names and address. They included a dollar bill for return postage. They also wrote a note promising a reward to the finder. At last they were ready. They cast the bottle into the waves.

Months passed. Nobody wrote to the Peckhams to claim the reward. The couple all but forgot about the bottle and its message.

Over three years later, Nguyen Van Hoa found the Peckham's message. It had traveled over 9,000 miles. Hoa saw the bottle floating in the South China Sea. Desperate with thirst, he had fished the bottle from the waves. He hoped it would contain something that he and his companions could drink.

Hoa had been an officer with the South Vietnamese army. When South Vietnam fell, he was captured. His enemies took him to a prison camp.

Life was hard in the prison camp. Guards forced Hoa to work long hours cutting timber. Sometimes he had to dig irrigation ditches. It was slave labor.

Torture and beating by the prison guards were routine. The only food Hoa received was small rations of rice and corn. On lucky days he could add to this diet. He caught insects, small rodents, and snakes. And he ate them.

Hoa endured this life for four years. Then he and his brother managed to escape. For a while they hid in Ho Chi Minh City. They were always afraid they would be discovered. If that happened, they would be returned to prison. They feared for their lives.

One day Hoa got himself and his brother onto a fishing boat. Its captain illegally carried refugees to Thailand. On Hoa's voyage, thirty people were crammed onto the boat. The craft had been designed to hold five. Living conditions were almost unbearable.

There was little food or water. When Hoa spotted the drift bottle, he was elated. But his hopes soon sank. The bottle contained nothing potable. However, Hoa recognized the American dollar. And the message inside the bottle gave him hope.

Luckily, Hoa's boat reached Thailand. He, his future wife, and his brother had survived. They went to a United Nations refugee camp. There they received food and shelter. It was there that Hoa wrote a note to the Peckhams. He told them of his past hardships. He wrote of his need to find freedom.

The Peckhams were stunned when they received Hoa's letter. Over three years had passed since they had launched the drift bottle. They had not expected to hear from a Vietnamese refugee.

For two years they wrote to Hoa at the refugee camp. They sent him money. They sent him gifts when his first child was born.

Finally, Hoa asked the Peckhams to sponsor him in America. This meant finding the family a place to live. It meant helping them learn to speak English. It meant helping them to find jobs.

The Peckhams decided to do this. They felt that fate had carried their bottle to worthy people.

"We felt the bottle ended up as it did for a reason," Dottie Peckham said.

Hoa and his family came to California. It was a time of joy. The family was truly free for the first time in over ten years.

The Peckhams found an apartment for the Hoas in Los Angeles. They helped the family furnish it. The Catholic Welfare Bureau helped Hoa pay the rent. Hoa immediately enrolled in a crash course in English. He knew this would help him in getting a job.

The Peckham's message bottle had not told what reward would be given. The Hoa family considered their reward priceless. They had received friendship, freedom, and a chance for a new life.

MAKING YOUR OWN DRIFT BOTTLE

Would you like to launch a drift bottle? Would you like a pen pal from another state or country? Or perhaps you'd like a surprise call from someone in your own city. A drift bottle could bring surprises to your doorstep.

Message bottles can be launched in any stream, river or ocean. The choice is yours.

If you live inland, study the rivers in your area. Rivers are active. They are always going someplace. Small streams flow into larger streams. Larger streams flow into rivers. And rivers flow into the sea.

You might want to trace the flow of water in a nearby stream. Start by finding this stream on a city or county map. From there, follow the stream's flow to a river. Locate the river on a state map. The river may flow through several states before it reaches the sea.

Think about this research. Can you see that a bottle tossed into a stream can reach the ocean?

Now it's time to create a seaworthy drift bottle. You can do little to make someone find your bottle. However, you can do a lot to assure that it will remain afloat.

Use a bottle with a screw-top cap. A catsup bottle or a pickle bottle will do very well. Catsup bottles are especially practical. They are made of very sturdy glass.

To be sure your bottle will float, test it. Cap the bottle first. Then submerge it in a bucket of water. Observe what happens. If the cap is loose, water will seep in. Check for leaks. Leave your bottle in the bucket for several hours. If it remains dry, all is well. If your bottle leaks, discard it and try another.

Floating bottles are more likely to survive if they contain some weight. This weight is called ballast. Ballast makes bottles travel better in the water. It's a good idea to partly fill your bottle with sand. You'll have to experiment with the amount needed. Stop adding sand when the bottle is about three-fourths submerged.

When your bottle floats in a suitable way, add your message. Include your name, your address and your telephone number. If you want to promise a reward, do so. But be prepared to pay if someone finds your message. A stamped postcard will make it easy for the finder to reply. It's a good idea to enclose one.

Once the ballast and your message are inside the bottle, seal it. Then coat the cap with wax. Your parents should help you with this part of your project. An old candle may be used for wax.

It is dangerous to melt wax over direct heat. A double-boiler system should be used. With an adult helping, place water in a small pan. Bring it to a boil. Drop pieces of candle wax into a tin can. Set this can in the boiling water. In a few minutes the wax will melt.

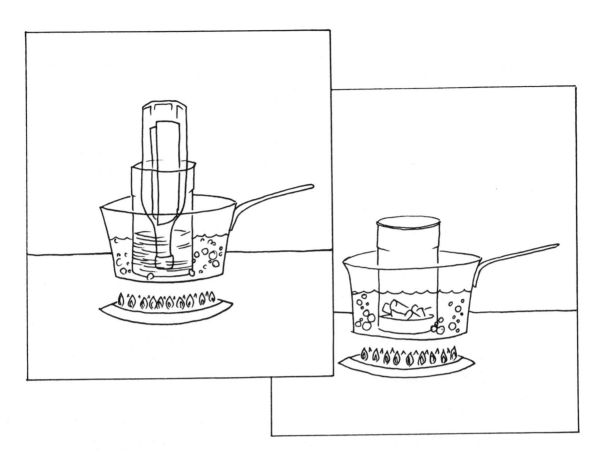

Holding your bottle upside down, insert it in the melted wax. Be sure the bottle cap and neck are well coated. Then remove the bottle from the wax. Let this thin coat of wax cool and dry. You may want to repeat this process several times. This will make the seal stronger.

Now, you are ready to place the bottle in the water. You could toss it into a river from a bridge. Or you could throw it into the sea from a boat.

Don't drop your bottle too near a shoreline. It could be caught in roots, branches, or rocks. You might find it yourself on your next trip to that shore.

So take care in preparing your drift bottle. Place it in the biggest expanse of flowing water near you. And wait. The waters of the world promise no exact delivery date. But in time they will return what has been given to them.

Good luck!

12 *A Note on the Environment*

Drift bottles have played a unique and interesting role in history. Their use today continues to provide us with scientific information.

A true drift bottle has a purpose. Bottles should not be thrown into a river or the sea as a matter of routine. This is a form of pollution.

If you decide to create and launch a drift bottle, be sure to have an educational or scientific purpose.

Use glass for your drift bottle as suggested in chapter eleven. Certain kinds of plastic refuse in the ocean have been found to cause injury or death to marine life. Plastic bags, in particular, are mistaken for jellyfish by some forms of marine life and ingested as food.

Be responsible to your environment. Plan your drift bottle experiments carefully. And have a purpose. Good luck.

- THE EDITOR -

DRIFT BOTTLES
in History and Folklore

BIBLIOGRAPHY

A BOTTLE COLLECTOR'S BOOK, Bob and Pat Ferraro, Western Printing and Publishing Co., Sparks, Nevada, 1966

THE PAST IN GLASS, Bob and Pat Ferraro, Western Printing and Publishing Co., Sparks, Nevada, 1964

THE BOTTLE BOOK, Adams, John P., New Hampshire Publishing Co., Somersworth, 1972

BOTTLE BONANZA, Beare, Nikki, Hurricane House Publishers Inc., 14301 S.W. 87th Ave., Miami, Florida, 1965

OLD BOTTLES FOUND ALONG FLORIDA KEYS, Monroe, Loretta, Wake-Brook House, Coral Gables, Florida, 1967

Periodicals:

"Drift Bottle Update" [1981-1982 Pacific Ocean Launch], National Geographic World, October, 1987

"Message in a Bottle," People Weekly, May 27, 1985

DRIFT BOTTLE RECORD

Launch Location: _____

_____

_____

Date: _____
Time: _____
Weather Conditions: _____

_____

_____

Date Returned: _____
Notes: _____

_____

_____

_____

_____

_____

_____

_____

_____

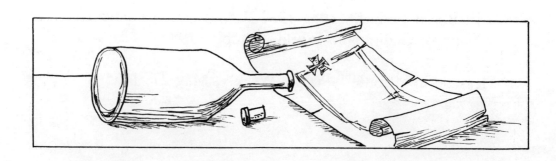

DRIFT BOTTLE RECORD

Launch Location: _____

_____

_____

Date: _____

Time: _____

Weather Conditions: _____

_____

_____

_____

Date Returned: _____

Notes: _____

_____

_____

_____

_____

_____

_____

_____

DRIFT BOTTLE RECORD

Launch Location: _____

_____

_____

Date: _____
Time: _____
Weather Conditions: _____

_____

_____

_____

Date Returned: _____
Notes: _____

_____

_____

_____

_____

_____

_____

_____

_____

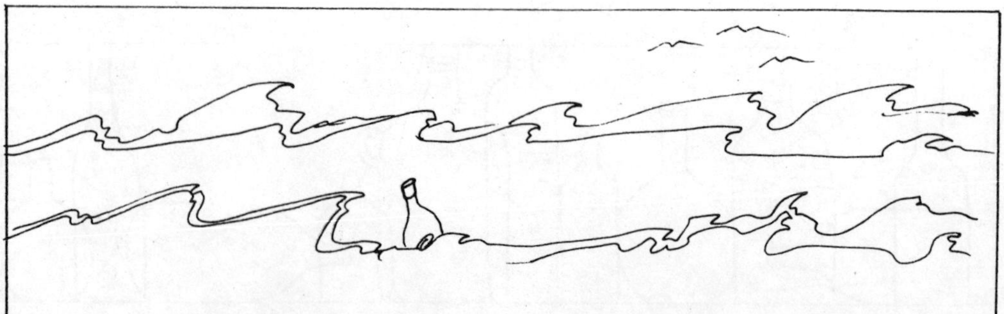